CW01261642

This journal belongs to

Lisa Folkard
T: 07854 418361
E: lisa.folkard@btinternet.com

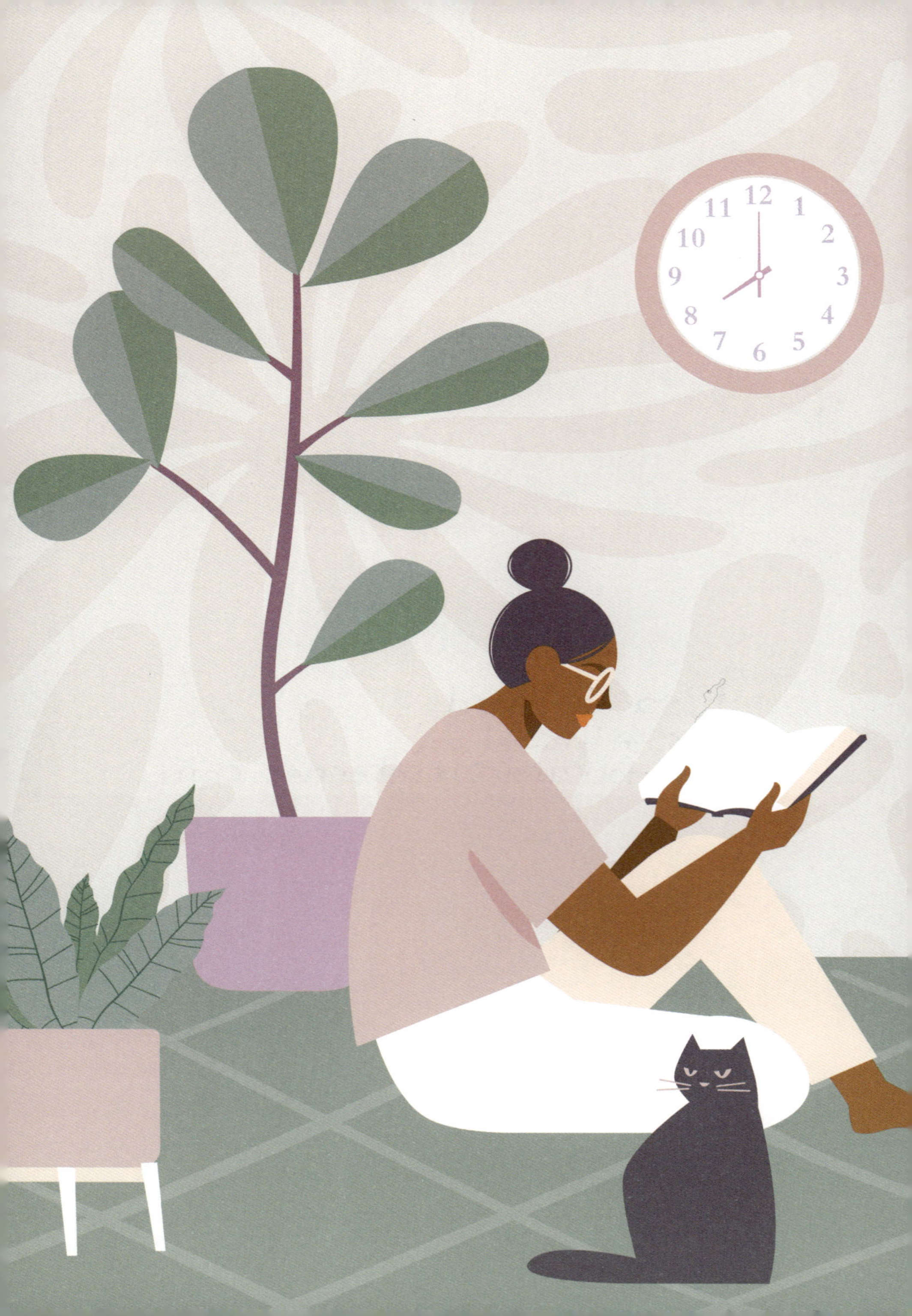

12
1
2
3
4
5
6
7
8
9
10
11

Budgeting
Journal

As many of us face an ongoing cost of living crisis, it can be harder and harder to feel in control of your finances. Spending can be all too easy with contactless and online payments, and even small purchases can soon add up to a significant figure when made every day or week. Saving, on the other hand, can seem harder and harder when we face rising bills.

The Budgeting Journal is here to help. By making a note of all your spending you will be able to clearly see where your money is going and identify potential areas where you can make savings. This journal will also help you to focus on your financial goals and keep track of your progress, whether you want to budget more effectively, cut back on non-essential spending, or if you are saving up for a large purchase or special occasion.

By picking up this journal, you are taking the first step towards being in better control of your money. We hope you find it to be a useful tool for your budgeting needs. Now, let's get started!

Contents

INTRODUCTION

10   Get started with budgeting

12   Your financial priorities

16   9 money-saving tips

20   Plan your saving goals

YOUR JOURNAL

26   How to use the journal

28   Spending categories

30   Bill schedule

34   Weekly budget diary

REVIEW & REFLECT

140   How to complete the monthly totals

142   Your monthly totals

166   Annual review

172   Reflect on your progress

Introduction

10 GET STARTED WITH BUDGETING

Discover the benefits of journaling for your budgeting needs

12 YOUR FINANCIAL PRIORITIES

Identify your spending habits and attitude to money

16 9 MONEY-SAVING TIPS

Helpful advice for your budgeting journey… plus what to avoid!

20 PLAN YOUR SAVING GOALS

Set yourself targets for the future to keep yourself on track

GETTING STARTED

✸ Get started ✸ with budgeting

Discover the benefits of creating a budget,
and how to use this book to keep you on track

Welcome to your new Budgeting Journal. This is your essential resource to help you keep account of your accounts! If you're new to budgeting, we will guide you through everything you need to know to create a budget, identify your financial priorities, set some goals for your spending and saving, and highlight where your money is going.

Creating a budget for your income has never been more important. There is a cost-of-living crisis happening around the world, with no indications that things will improve quickly. Therefore, it pays to be prepared, as the prices of utilities, rents and mortgages, childcare, services and transport are trending upwards quarter on quarter. Your budget starts simply, with your total monthly income (after tax deductions) minus all your fixed, non-negotiable payments. What you're left with is what you have to budget for everything else. By taking charge of your money, you can work towards saving, reducing debt and preventing overspending.

There are many apps that offer budgeting tools and resources, some that even automate a lot of the process by linking to your bank accounts, but there are advantages to writing down your spending and budget. Putting pen to paper is a very deliberate action, and one that makes you think. It gives you a moment's pause to think about what you are spending and why. It's also very easy to flick through all your transactions in one go to keep you on track.

For this Budgeting Journal to work for you, the most important thing is honesty and transparency. This means writing down every single financial transaction you make. Your fixed expenses are straightforward and may not change hugely from month to month. It's the day-to-day spending that can often end up blowing a budget – that cup of coffee on the run, a quick snack, impulse buys at the checkout… In the era of contactless payments, it's all too easy to swipe your card or phone and forget that it's real money, with a real impact, that you're using.

> **66** In the era of contactless payments, it's all too easy to swipe your card or phone and forget that it's real money **99**

Writing down your spending helps to create a more tangible response to what you're buying.

You may find yourself questioning your purchases, deliberating more, and actively looking for lower-cost alternatives. We make so many financial decisions each week without any thought; writing down your spending brings forward a more mindful approach to money.

To get started, work your way through this introductory section. You will find top tips and advice, as well as practical activities to help you get on top of your current financial situation. Try not to worry if you feel overwhelmed or scared by seeing your numbers written down – this is just your starting point. No matter where you are now, over the course of the next 12 months, you can regain control of your finances and work towards your personal finance goals.

Throughout the rest of the journal, you will find pages to help you track your monthly bills and outgoings, your weekly spending, your monthly and yearly spending totals, and more. We recommend that you spend a little time reading the 'How to' sections to get the most out of these trackers.

If you're ready to enter the world of budgeting, let's get cracking!

GETTING STARTED

Your financial
✶ priorities ✶

We all have different approaches and behaviours around spending; identifying yours can help you to get on top of your budgeting goals

---

When it comes to setting a budget, there is no 'one-size-fits-all' solution. We're all different people, with different budgets and different priorities. What you consider to be an essential in your daily life may not be so important to someone else. Some of this comes down to circumstance, and some is personal preference. By identifying your own financial priorities and your attitudes to spending, you will be able to come up with your own goals, plans and spending criteria.

There are certain spendings that are a priority for everyone, and these are your non-negotiable bills and outgoings. Your fixed expenditure includes things like your rent or mortgage repayments, childcare costs, utility bills and so on. After that, what you spend your remaining budget on can mostly be split into 'essentials' and 'non-essentials'.

Essentials are the things that you have to spend your money on in your day-to-day life. Transport is often an essential, though what kind of transport will depend on the individual. If you need a car, running costs will be essential; if you use public transport to commute to work, then the cost of tickets will be an essential. However, if you want to upgrade to a first-class train ticket for a journey, then that is a non-essential purchase.

> 66 What you spend your remaining budget on can mostly be split into 'essentials' and 'non-essentials' 99

Non-essentials are those things that you would like, rather than need. It is important to budget for these non-essentials that matter to you, as being too strict with your finances can lead to splurges, or anxiety over spending at all.

Determining your essentials versus non-essentials will depend on many factors. People working from home, for example, will have different requirements (such as investing in office furniture and better broadband) to those working in an office (business attire, commuting costs and so on). Your family set-up will also make a difference, whether you have children, older parents or pets to care for, which all come with additional and necessary costs. We've provided you with space to write your own list of essentials and non-essentials in this section.

When thinking about your essentials, don't forget to include any unavoidable future costs that come up regularly that you need to plan for, such as birthdays, Christmas, car MOTs and the like. When you know you have big-cost events coming up, it's a good idea to save for these month on month, rather than trying to find the money when the occasion arises. These are often referred to as 'sinking funds', where you save a bit of money regularly over time in order to pay for future costs. You may wish to include sinking funds in your savings goals and targets.

ESSENTIALS VS NON-ESSENTIALS

In the table below, identify your most common essential and non-essential spending categories. Many will be obvious, but others will depend on your particular circumstances – take clothing, for example: parents regularly need new clothes for young children as they grow (essential), whereas adults with wardrobes full of perfectly good outfits don't *need* more (non-essential).

ESSENTIALS	NON-ESSENTIALS

> **When thinking about your financial priorities, don't forget to include some things that bring you joy**

Next, you will need to think about the way that you spend. Are you quite impulsive? Do you spend out of habit? Read through the 'personality' types on page 15 to find out which spending characteristics you have. An awareness of how you spend can help when it comes to planning your budget – for example, if you know you are an emotional spender, then you need to have strategies in place to help you cope with your emotions in other ways.

Similarly, what kind of saver are you? You might be a regular saver, a sporadic saver, or not currently save at all. Consider what you do now and what you would like to do in the future. Savings can be for a number of different things, both short term and long term, and you will have the opportunity to think about these in more detail over the next couple of sections of this journal.

When thinking about your financial priorities, don't forget to include some things that bring you joy. It's great if you want to think about future occasions, plan for retirement, save for something big like a new car or a house deposit and so on. But give yourself a little freedom and flexibility to live in the now as well; this is the best thing about a budget – it's yours to mould however you like. And with careful planning and accountability, you can pay for your essentials, save for your future goals, and have some fun along the way too.

What type of spender are you?

When trying to take control of your finances, it is helpful to recognise your attitudes to spending and whether you have any counterproductive habits to address. Do you see yourself in these common spending 'personalities'?

EMOTIONAL	IMPULSIVE
Your emotions, rather than your wallet, influence your spending. You find yourself buying things to boost your mood or alleviate boredom, regardless of whether it is a sensible financial decision. **SIGNS:** Regretting purchases or feeling disappointed; having lots of items you don't really want or need. **TIPS:** Try to wait at least 24 hours before making non-essential purchases (you may reconsider). Learn to recognise/acknowledge the emotions driving your behaviour. In serious cases, a professional therapist may help you understand and deal with the root causes.	Similar to emotional spending, but less influenced by mood – you frequently make purchases on a whim, such as seeing something on offer, regardless of whether you need it or can afford it. **SIGNS:** Regretting purchases; having lots of items you don't want or need; a sense that you will 'miss out' if you don't buy an item immediately. **TIPS:** Try to wait at least 24 hours before making non-essential purchases (you may reconsider). Leave cards at home and only carry the cash you need, or have a separate 'spending' account from your main account to limit overspending.
HABITUAL	CONTROLLED
You make regular purchases out of habit without considering their impact on your budget. These may also be tied in to your social life, such as regular drinks with friends, or stem from a need to stay on trend with the latest fashion or tech. **SIGNS:** Denial over how much is actually spent on 'the little things'; trying to justify non-essential purchases by claiming that they are essential. **TIPS:** To help put things into perspective, calculate how much these 'small' purchases add up to over a year. A daily £2 takeaway coffee, for example, will cost you over £700 a year!	You are hyperaware of what you are spending and disciplined with your finances. However, in some cases you may actually find it hard to part with your money, even when you can afford to. **SIGNS:** Anxiety over unplanned or excessive spending; feeling worried/guilty about overspend; indecisiveness/hesitance over major purchases. **TIPS:** If you are financially stable but still stress over everyday spending, trust your budgeting abilities and try to take a more relaxed approach. Being a controlled spender is a positive skill, but don't let spending control you!

GETTING STARTED

✳ 9 money-saving tips ✳

Get on top of your budget and start saving with these simple tips and tricks

---

1. TRACK YOUR SPENDING

You need to get into the habit of tracking every single penny you spend. Not just the big outgoings or more significant purchases, but even the small daily purchases, like a cup of coffee or a packet of chewing gum. If you're out and about and don't have this journal with you, ask for receipts so you can track everything when you get home, or write it down immediately in the Notes app on your phone or a small notebook. This journal has space for you to write your weekly expenditure down, so make it part of your evening routine to review your day and log all of your spending.

2. FOLLOW THE 50/30/20 RULE

The 50/30/20 budgeting rule is a ratio split of how you should ideally spend your income. 50% of your income should go to your essential payments, such as rent/mortgage, bills, groceries, loan repayments and so on. Then 30% of your income is for living your life, which might be socialising, taking day trips, shopping for non-essentials and so on. The final 20% is for saving and investing, which means repaying debt, building an emergency fund or putting money aside for a specific future goal. Don't worry if this ratio isn't possible for you right now; you can adjust the numbers to suit your present situation and work towards it.

3. REVIEW YOUR BILLS

So many of us 'set and forget' our bills – they go out every month automatically without much thought. However, it pays to set aside time once a month to go through your bills and review what you're paying. Keep a note of renewal dates and then make sure you check if you're getting the best deals you can. This is especially true of things like insurance (car, home) and services (internet, phone bill), where shopping around can save you a fair amount of money. Use a price comparison site to see what offers are available to you, and keep an eye out for any bonus incentives for switching providers.

4. COOLING-OFF PERIOD

When you take on a financial commitment, like a loan or 'pay later' offer, as a consumer you have the right to a cooling-off period in case you change your mind. Try to apply this to your non-essential spending habits too. If you see something you want, don't buy it straight away. Set yourself a cooling-off period first – this could be a few days if it's time limited, or a month. Then, at the end of the cooling-off period, ask yourself if it's still something you want and consider if it fits into your budget. You can then either make the purchase, knowing you've really thought about it, or you can choose not to buy the item this time.

5. LEARN TO SAY NO

If you find you're constantly being asked out for social events, dinners, lunches, day trips, weekends away and so on, don't forget that you can say no. It can be hard if that 'fear of missing out' kicks in, or if you feel obliged to attend. Set yourself a budget for these kinds of costs and prioritise those things you'll enjoy the most. If you want to socialise but it's outside your budget, then you could suggest lower-cost activities instead: 'I'd love to see you for dinner, but why don't you come to mine instead of going out. I'll cook, then we can catch up.'

6. SET SOME GOALS

Having a goal can keep you focused and motivated on saving money. It's good to have both short-term and long-term goals in your savings plan. In the next section of this journal, we'll be talking you through how to set your goals and why it's important to do so. Make sure you track your progress towards your savings goals, and keep the money in a separate pot from your day-to-day spending funds. You can set spending goals as well, such as decreasing your weekly food bill or finding the lowest-priced fuel in your local area.

7. REPAIR, REUSE, RECYCLE

Get out of the habit of buying new when something breaks, and try to reduce your waste. You will often find that it's cheaper to repair something than it is to replace it – a new screen on your phone is far less costly than a brand new phone, for example. Try to find new uses for things you've finished with; there are some great hacks online for reusing common household items. Check out local Facebook recycling groups, where you can often pick up things for free that others don't need anymore, and explore the growing world of second-hand shopping.

8. AUTOMATE YOUR SAVINGS

Make sure that your planned savings are moved from your main account automatically when you've been paid. That way, you can't be tempted to save less than you planned (unless you need to) or dip into it through overspending. Set up a standing order to move your money into a savings account or separate pot. You can also get automatic savings apps and tools that offer things like 'round-ups' where your purchases are rounded up and the difference put into savings. It might only be a small amount, but it adds up over time. Do your research to see if it's right for you.

9. PLAN IN 'NO-SPEND' DAYS

At the start of each month, when you're setting your budget and doing your financial admin, try to plan in plenty of no-spend days. Apart from essential, planned purchases, on these days you should aim to spend nothing. No trips to the shop, no lunches out, no coffees on the run... the reason it's good to plan the days in advance is so that you're prepared with what you need for the day, such as food and drink, to limit the chance you'll have to make an emergency purchase. Set yourself a target number of no-spend days per month.

HABITS TO AVOID

Bad spending habits can derail us in our savings goals. Here are some of the most common:

SPENDING AS SOON AS YOU'RE PAID
At the end of the month, do you start planning what you want to buy when money comes in? Then spend it all in the first week? Try to set a weekly spending limit so you have money throughout the month.

BUYING RATHER THAN MAKING MEALS
So much money is spent on food outside the home, which costs a lot! It's much cheaper to prepare food and drink at home to take with us.

SUBSCRIPTIONS
Many apps will ask you to subscribe to access content. Usually, you get hooked with a free trial, but then forget to cancel and end up paying. Set yourself reminders and do regular subscription audits.

IMPULSE BUYING
Retailers are wise to impulse buying and know how to trigger a spending response. If you pick up an unplanned purchase, take a minute to ask yourself, 'Do I really need this?'

ALWAYS HAVING THE LATEST TECH
It seems like as soon as we buy a phone/tablet/watch, it's already out of date. But your phone is fine; it will last you ages – if it's functional and does what *you* need it to do, don't rush to upgrade.

GETTING STARTED

✶ Plan your ✶ saving goals

Stay motivated and on track by setting clear
financial goals within your budget

Savings can give you more power and control over your money, but saving with no specific goal in mind can make it harder to stay on track. By setting a goal, it helps to give you a clearer picture of what the money is for and why you want to save it. You're more likely to make sacrifices in your day-to-day budget to prioritise saving if you know it's for a good reason.

Goals can be split into different categories. Short-term goals are those that you hope to achieve within the next few years, which might be things like a dream holiday, a deposit for your first house or a new car. Then you have more medium-term goals, which are things that you know are coming up in the next decade but are not imminent. If you have children, for example, this might be saving for their higher education, or you might be looking at changing your career, travelling or relocating. Next, you have long-term goals, which involve planning for your future in the form of things like a pension or retirement plan. On top of all of this, you will probably want to consider ongoing objectives, which could include things like maintaining an emergency fund for if things go wrong, or saving for regular, costly events like holidays and birthdays.

These goals should be personal. Take some time to think about what is important to you. Consider what you want your life to look like a year from now, five years

> ❝ You will probably want to think about ongoing savings, like having an emergency fund if things go wrong ❞

from now, a decade from now, and in your later life. This will help you to identify your priorities, which will help you start to lay out some initial objectives.

When setting goals, you want to try to make them SMART: Specific, Measurable, Achievable, Relevant and Time-Bound. The SMART system provides context and relevance for your goals, which helps keep you motivated. Specific means that you need to really drill down into what you are saving for, rather than a generic, 'I want to save money for the future'. This might be something like, 'Buy a house in [a specific year]'. Then you want it to be Measurable, which you can do by working out how much you need to save and by when, then breaking that down into yearly, monthly and weekly savings targets. You can easily track whether you're ahead of, behind, or on target. Your goal needs to be Achievable – if you set your savings target too high, you will struggle to keep up with it. Consider how much money you can comfortably set aside, while still being able to live your life in the now. Your goals should be Relevant – don't set a savings goal just because you feel that you 'should'; your aims should be tailored to your life and what you want to achieve. Finally, your goals should be Time-Bound, which means setting a deadline date so you can see the endpoint to encourage you to stay on track.

However, you do need a little flexibility in your goals too. Our financial health changes throughout our lives; unexpected events can come out of the blue (global pandemics, recession, job losses, critical illness, and so on) and ruin best-made plans. If that happens, you will need to reassess and set new goals.

Setting goals is an important step – identifying SMART goals and regularly assessing your progress will help keep you on track

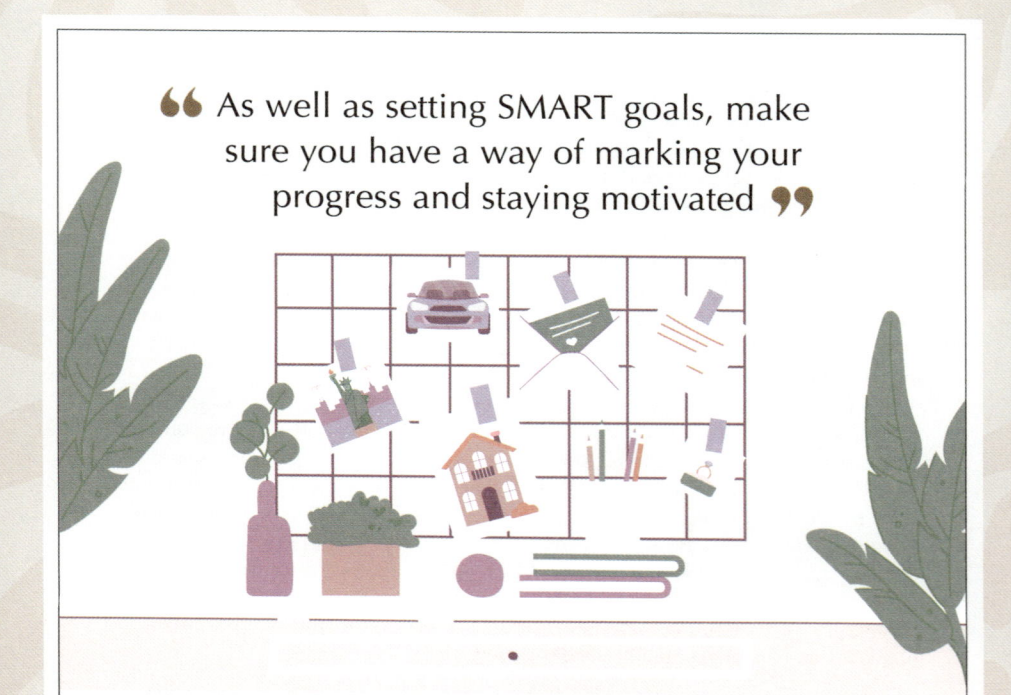

> ❝ As well as setting SMART goals, make sure you have a way of marking your progress and staying motivated ❞

As well as setting SMART goals, you need to make sure you have a way of marking your progress and staying motivated. Different people are motivated in different ways. If you are saving for something that is important to you, but it means making a few cuts in the short term, having a vision board might help. This can be cuttings, photos, maps, quotes… whatever you like that represents your eventual goal to help you stay on track. Keep this somewhere you can see it.

You might be more motivated by a data-based tracking system, where you can update regularly with how much you have saved towards your target, with a percentage of how close you are to your goal. You might feel like you are getting nowhere, but seeing the numbers clearly will help you see how far you've come.

You will need to set a little time aside regularly – many people do it monthly, particularly if it ties in around payday – to review your goals, update your totals and make any amendments. Getting into this habit helps you to stay accountable. If you've fallen behind for any reason, you have a chance to think about whether this is a one-off due to circumstance and can be made up, or whether your goal is not achievable and needs to be tweaked. Once you have some goals in place, you can set up the practicalities. This means organising standing orders into your savings accounts, delegating your money when it comes in, and actioning any payments you need to make.

It can seem overwhelming if you've never done anything like this before, but you can start with small goals and build up as your financial confidence grows.

My goals

List your personal financial goals below. Include any target dates if these are relevant, such as saving up for a specific event.

SHORT TERM (UP TO 5 YEARS)	MEDIUM TERM (5-10 YEARS)
Buy a new car	Decorate home
Holiday every year	New carpets
New sofa	New bed

LONG TERM (10+ YEARS)	ONGOING (NOT DATE-SPECIFIC, SUCH AS HABITS TO DEVELOP)
Funeral plan	

Your Journal

26   HOW TO USE THE JOURNAL
A quick guide to making the most of the journal pages

28   SPENDING CATEGORIES
Some ideas to help with your spending breakdown analysis

30   BILL SCHEDULE
Use this handy calendar to track all your bills and regular payments

34   WEEKLY BUDGET DIARY
A 52-week journal to note down all your spending and saving

JOURNAL GUIDE

How to use the journal

The following section contains a year's worth of budgeting pages ready to help you keep track of your spending each week. Here are some tips on how to complete each section…

1 BALANCES & TARGETS

At the start of each week, use the Balances section to list the current state of your main accounts, including credit cards and debts. If you have spending and/or saving targets for the week, you can also add these at the top of the table for reference.

2 MAIN TABLE

Here is where you will add the details of your income and spending throughout the week. See pages 28-29 for more information on categories and some ideas for options you could use. Income will typically be your salary, but don't forget to include things like refunds, money gifts, and repayments from people.

> 66 If you get paid monthly, you may prefer to divide your salary up into a series of weekly allowances 99

3 SPENDING TOTALS

Add up everything in the 'in' column of the main table for your total income, and everything in the 'out' column for your total weekly spend. Take the 'out' total away from your 'in' total for your net income – if the value is negative, you have spent more than you have earned that week. If you get paid monthly, you may prefer to divide your salary up into a series of weekly allowances rather than list the lump sum.

4 CATEGORY SUBTOTALS

Add up the total spend for each of the categories you have used this week. Remember to take into account any income for the categories (such as refunds or repayments), if relevant, to reflect your actual spend.

5 NOTES

Use this section to add any comments or reminders for the week, or to use as extra space for any of the other sections if you run out of room.

JOURNAL GUIDE

✴ Spending categories ✴

Not only is it important to keep track of how much you are spending, you should also be mindful of *how* you are spending it

---

On the right are some suggestions for categories you might want to use throughout this journal. It is up to you how broad or specific you choose to go with your categories – the more specific areas you use, the easier it will be to track essential versus non-essential spending if that is something you need to focus on. For example, you could use the generic 'food/drink' to keep things simple, or you could separate purchases into 'groceries' (essential), takeaways (non-essential) and so on. The most important thing is to ensure your categories fit in with your lifestyle and goals.

A NOTE ON CREDIT CARDS

Depending on how you use your credit card, you may need to include your card spend in a different way. If you always pay off your credit card *in full* every month, you can treat your card transactions just like normal spending, and the credit card figure in your 'Balances' section is not necessary. However, if you don't pay off your credit card in full, you will need to consider it a debt and take any applicable interest into account. Make sure you don't count credit card payments twice by including both the individual card purchases *and* the credit card bill when you pay it off – you should only use one or the other.

Category ideas

FOOD/DRINK
- Groceries
- Drinks / Alcohol
- Takeaways
- Coffee / Hot drinks
- Snacks
- Meals out
- Meal subscription services

BILLS
- Rent / Mortgage
- Electricity
- Gas
- Broadband
- Phone
- TV licence
- Council tax
- Insurance (home, car, health, travel, pet etc)
- Water / Sewerage
- Credit card interest and fees (see the note on p28)
- Debt repayments

TRAVEL
- Petrol / Charging
- Travel cards / Season tickets
- Parking fees
- Taxi fares
- Vehicle tax
- Vehicle service / MOT
- Vehicle repairs

EDUCATION
- Tuition fees
- Textbooks
- Software / Academic subscriptions

WORK
- Salary
- Freelance
- Bonus
- Expenses
- Benefits / Welfare payments

HOME
- Furniture
- Homeware / Décor
- Home essentials (lightbulbs, cleaning supplies etc)
- DIY
- Gardening
- Trades / Services / Repairs
- Renovations

HEALTH/BEAUTY
- Toiletries
- Medicine / Prescriptions
- Gym / PT / Fitness classes
- Hairdresser / Haircare
- Spa / Beauty treatments
- Makeup / Premium skincare

FAMILY
- Childcare
- Clothes / Uniforms
- Toys
- Children's activities / Trips
- School equipment
- Pet care

APPAREL
- Clothes
- Shoes
- Accessories
- Outerwear / Sportswear

ENTERTAINMENT
- Tech / Gadgets
- TV / Streaming services
- Music / Streaming services
- Games
- Books
- Activities (cinema, museums, concerts etc)
- Nights out

ADMIN
- Refunds
- Postage
- Printing
- Stationery

HOLIDAYS
- Transport (flights, trains, ferries, taxis etc)
- Accommodation
- Meals / Drinks
- Holiday activities
- Visas
- Currency / Exchange fees

OTHER

Bill schedule

	Bill	Due date	Amount
1	DVLA : Car Tax	1st	15.75
2	Axa : Car Insurance	5th	37.05
3	Apple.com : Storage	6th	2.99
4	Amazon : Audible	8th	7.99
5	Sky : TV + Broadband	8th	
6	Amazon : Prime	12th	8.99
7	Dad : Mobile Phone	4 weekly	35.00
8	Liz : Holiday Loan	4 weekly	100.00
9	Hughes Rental	4 weekly	20.00
10	British Gas : E	2 weekly	
11	British Gas : G	2 weekly	
12	HMCTS : Fine	2 weekly	
13	Anglian Water		
14	TV Licence		
15			
16			
17			
18			
19			

	JAN	FEB	MAR	APR	MAY	JUN	JUL	AUG	SEP	OCT	NOV	DEC
				TICK ALL OF THE MONTHS EACH BILL IS DUE								
	✓	✓	✓	✓	✓	✓	✓	✓	✓	✓	✓	✓
	✓	✓	✓	✓	✓	✓	✓	✓				
	✓	✓	✓	✓	✓	✓	✓	✓	✓	✓	✓	✓
	✓	✓	✓									
	✓	✓	✓	✓	✓	✓	✓	✓	✓	✓	✓	✓
	✓	✓	✓	✓	✓	✓	✓	✓	✓	✓	✓	✓
	✓	✓	✓	✓	✓	✓	✓	✓	✓	✓	✓	✓
	—	✓	✓	✓								
	✓	✓	✓	✓	✓	✓	✓	✓	✓	✓	✓	✓
	✓	✓	✓	✓	✓	✓	✓	✓	✓	✓	✓	✓
	✓	✓	✓	✓	✓	✓	✓	✓	✓	✓	✓	✓
	✓	✓	✓	✓	✓	✓						

TRACK YOUR OUTGOINGS

✶ Bill schedule ✶

	Bill	Due date	Amount	
20				
21				
22				
23				
24				
25				
26				
27				
28				
29				
30				
31				
32				
33				
34				
35				
36				
37				
38				

	JAN	FEB	MAR	APR	MAY	JUN	JUL	AUG	SEP	OCT	NOV	DEC
				TICK ALL OF THE MONTHS EACH BILL IS DUE								

WEEKLY BUDGET DIARY

✦ Week One ✦

Week beginning	Balances			
Friday 05.04.23	CURRENT ACCOUNT	CREDIT CARDS	SAVINGS	DEBTS
My money mood 🙂 😐 ☹️				

Targets _____ IN _____ OUT _____

DATE	DETAILS	CATEGORY	AMOUNT IN	AMOUNT OUT
05/04	DWP ESA	Direct	366.70	
	HMCTS Fine	Card	~~40.00~~	40.00
	Hughes Rental	Card	~~30.~~	30.00
	Cash			
	Garage/Fuel			
06/04	DWP PIP	Direct	380.00	
	Liz: Holiday	Direct		100.00
	Dad: Mobile	Direct		35.00
	British Gas: E	Card		
	British Gas: G	Card		

DATE	DETAILS	CATEGORY	AMOUNT	
			IN	OUT

Totals _____ IN _____ OUT _____ DIFFERENCE

Spending breakdown		Notes
CATEGORY	SUBTOTAL	

WEEKLY BUDGET DIARY

✶ Week Two ✶

Week beginning	Balances			
	CURRENT ACCOUNT	CREDIT CARDS	SAVINGS	DEBTS
My money mood				
🙂 😐 🙁				

Targets _____ IN _____ OUT _____

DATE	DETAILS	CATEGORY	AMOUNT	
			IN	OUT

DATE	DETAILS	CATEGORY	AMOUNT	
			IN	OUT

Totals _____ IN _____ OUT _____ DIFFERENCE

Spending breakdown		Notes
CATEGORY	SUBTOTAL	

WEEKLY BUDGET DIARY

✶ Week Three ✶

Week beginning	Balances			
	CURRENT ACCOUNT	CREDIT CARDS	SAVINGS	DEBTS
My money mood 🙂 😐 ☹️				

Targets _____ IN _____ OUT _____

DATE	DETAILS	CATEGORY	AMOUNT	
			IN	OUT

DATE	DETAILS	CATEGORY	AMOUNT	
			IN	OUT

Totals   IN   OUT   DIFFERENCE

Spending breakdown		Notes
CATEGORY	SUBTOTAL	

Week Four

WEEKLY BUDGET DIARY

Week beginning	Balances			
	CURRENT ACCOUNT	CREDIT CARDS	SAVINGS	DEBTS
My money mood :) :| :(				

Targets _____ IN _____ OUT

DATE	DETAILS	CATEGORY	AMOUNT	
			IN	OUT

DATE	DETAILS	CATEGORY	AMOUNT	
			IN	OUT

Totals .... IN .... OUT .... DIFFERENCE

Spending breakdown		Notes
CATEGORY	SUBTOTAL	

WEEKLY BUDGET DIARY

✶ Week Five ✶

Week beginning	Balances			
	CURRENT ACCOUNT	CREDIT CARDS	SAVINGS	DEBTS
My money mood ☺ 😐 ☹				

Targets　　　　　　　IN　　　　　　　　OUT

DATE	DETAILS	CATEGORY	AMOUNT	
			IN	OUT

DATE	DETAILS	CATEGORY	AMOUNT	
			IN	OUT

Totals _____ IN _____ OUT _____ DIFFERENCE

Spending breakdown

CATEGORY	SUBTOTAL

Notes

WEEKLY BUDGET DIARY

✷ Week Six ✷

Week beginning	Balances			
	CURRENT ACCOUNT	CREDIT CARDS	SAVINGS	DEBTS
My money mood ☺ 😐 ☹				

Targets _____ IN _____ OUT _____

DATE	DETAILS	CATEGORY	AMOUNT	
			IN	OUT

DATE	DETAILS	CATEGORY	AMOUNT	
			IN	OUT

Totals   IN   OUT   DIFFERENCE

Spending breakdown		Notes
CATEGORY	SUBTOTAL	

WEEKLY BUDGET DIARY

✳ Week Seven ✳

Week beginning	Balances			
	CURRENT ACCOUNT	CREDIT CARDS	SAVINGS	DEBTS
My money mood ☺ 😐 ☹				

Targets _____ IN _____ OUT

DATE	DETAILS	CATEGORY	AMOUNT	
			IN	OUT

DATE	DETAILS	CATEGORY	AMOUNT	
			IN	OUT

Totals   IN   OUT   DIFFERENCE

Spending breakdown		Notes
CATEGORY	SUBTOTAL	

WEEKLY BUDGET DIARY

✳ Week Eight ✳

Week beginning	Balances			
	CURRENT ACCOUNT	CREDIT CARDS	SAVINGS	DEBTS
My money mood 🙂 😐 ☹️				

Targets _____ IN _____ OUT _____

DATE	DETAILS	CATEGORY	AMOUNT	
			IN	OUT

DATE	DETAILS	CATEGORY	AMOUNT	
			IN	OUT

Totals .... IN .... OUT .... DIFFERENCE

Spending breakdown | Notes

CATEGORY	SUBTOTAL

WEEKLY BUDGET DIARY

✳ Week Nine ✳

Week beginning	Balances			
	CURRENT ACCOUNT	CREDIT CARDS	SAVINGS	DEBTS
My money mood ☺ 😐 ☹				

Targets   IN   OUT

DATE	DETAILS	CATEGORY	AMOUNT	
			IN	OUT

DATE	DETAILS	CATEGORY	AMOUNT	
			IN	OUT

Totals _____ IN _____ OUT _____ DIFFERENCE

Spending breakdown		Notes
CATEGORY	SUBTOTAL	

WEEKLY BUDGET DIARY

✶ Week Ten ✶

Week beginning	Balances			
	CURRENT ACCOUNT	CREDIT CARDS	SAVINGS	DEBTS
My money mood ☺ 😐 ☹				

Targets   IN   OUT

DATE	DETAILS	CATEGORY	AMOUNT	
			IN	OUT

DATE	DETAILS	CATEGORY	AMOUNT	
			IN	OUT

Totals _____ IN _____ OUT _____ DIFFERENCE

Spending breakdown		Notes
CATEGORY	SUBTOTAL	

WEEKLY BUDGET DIARY

✶ Week Eleven ✶

Week beginning	Balances			
	CURRENT ACCOUNT	CREDIT CARDS	SAVINGS	DEBTS
My money mood :) :| :(				

Targets _____ IN _____ OUT

DATE	DETAILS	CATEGORY	AMOUNT	
			IN	OUT

DATE	DETAILS	CATEGORY	AMOUNT	
			IN	OUT

Totals _____ IN _____ OUT _____ DIFFERENCE

Spending breakdown		Notes
CATEGORY	SUBTOTAL	

WEEKLY BUDGET DIARY

✳ Week Twelve ✳

Week beginning	Balances			
	CURRENT ACCOUNT	CREDIT CARDS	SAVINGS	DEBTS
My money mood ☺ 😐 ☹				

Targets _____ IN _____ OUT

DATE	DETAILS	CATEGORY	AMOUNT	
			IN	OUT

DATE	DETAILS	CATEGORY	AMOUNT	
			IN	OUT

Totals _____ IN _____ OUT _____ DIFFERENCE

Spending breakdown		Notes
CATEGORY	SUBTOTAL	

WEEKLY BUDGET DIARY

✶ Week Thirteen ✶

Week beginning	Balances			
	CURRENT ACCOUNT	CREDIT CARDS	SAVINGS	DEBTS
My money mood ☺ 😐 ☹				

Targets _____ IN _____ OUT

DATE	DETAILS	CATEGORY	AMOUNT	
			IN	OUT

DATE	DETAILS	CATEGORY	AMOUNT	
			IN	OUT

Totals   IN   OUT   DIFFERENCE

Spending breakdown		Notes
CATEGORY	SUBTOTAL	

WEEKLY BUDGET DIARY

Week Fourteen

Week beginning	Balances			
	CURRENT ACCOUNT	CREDIT CARDS	SAVINGS	DEBTS
My money mood ☺ 😐 ☹				

Targets _____ IN _____ OUT _____

DATE	DETAILS	CATEGORY	AMOUNT	
			IN	OUT

DATE	DETAILS	CATEGORY	AMOUNT	
			IN	OUT

Totals _____ IN _____ OUT _____ DIFFERENCE

Spending breakdown		Notes
CATEGORY	SUBTOTAL	

WEEKLY BUDGET DIARY

✶ Week Fifteen ✶

Week beginning	Balances				
	CURRENT ACCOUNT	CREDIT CARDS	SAVINGS	DEBTS
My money mood ☺ 😐 ☹				

Targets   IN   OUT

DATE	DETAILS	CATEGORY	AMOUNT	
			IN	OUT

DATE	DETAILS	CATEGORY	AMOUNT	
			IN	OUT

Totals _____ IN _____ OUT _____ DIFFERENCE

Spending breakdown		Notes
CATEGORY	SUBTOTAL	

Week Sixteen

Week beginning	Balances			
	CURRENT ACCOUNT	CREDIT CARDS	SAVINGS	DEBTS
My money mood				

Targets _____ IN _____ OUT

DATE	DETAILS	CATEGORY	AMOUNT	
			IN	OUT

DATE	DETAILS	CATEGORY	AMOUNT	
			IN	OUT

Totals　　　　　　　　　IN　　　　　　　　　OUT　　　　　　　　　DIFFERENCE

Spending breakdown		Notes
CATEGORY	SUBTOTAL	

WEEKLY BUDGET DIARY

Week Seventeen

Week beginning	Balances			
	CURRENT ACCOUNT	CREDIT CARDS	SAVINGS	DEBTS
My money mood ☺ 😐 ☹				

Targets _____ IN _____ OUT

DATE	DETAILS	CATEGORY	AMOUNT	
			IN	OUT

DATE	DETAILS	CATEGORY	AMOUNT	
			IN	OUT

Totals _____ IN _____ OUT _____ DIFFERENCE

Spending breakdown		Notes
CATEGORY	SUBTOTAL	

WEEKLY BUDGET DIARY

✦ Week Eighteen ✦

Week beginning	Balances			
	CURRENT ACCOUNT	CREDIT CARDS	SAVINGS	DEBTS
My money mood ☺ 😐 ☹				

Targets .... IN .... OUT

DATE	DETAILS	CATEGORY	AMOUNT	
			IN	OUT

DATE	DETAILS	CATEGORY	AMOUNT	
			IN	OUT

Totals .... IN .... OUT .... DIFFERENCE

Spending breakdown		Notes
CATEGORY	SUBTOTAL	

Week Nineteen

Week beginning	Balances			
	CURRENT ACCOUNT	CREDIT CARDS	SAVINGS	DEBTS
My money mood ☺ 😐 ☹				

Targets _____ IN _____ OUT _____

DATE	DETAILS	CATEGORY	AMOUNT	
			IN	OUT

DATE	DETAILS	CATEGORY	AMOUNT	
			IN	OUT

Totals .... IN .... OUT .... DIFFERENCE

Spending breakdown		Notes
CATEGORY	SUBTOTAL	

WEEKLY BUDGET DIARY

✶ Week Twenty ✶

Week beginning	Balances			
	CURRENT ACCOUNT	CREDIT CARDS	SAVINGS	DEBTS
My money mood ☺ ☹ ☹				

Targets   IN   OUT

DATE	DETAILS	CATEGORY	AMOUNT	
			IN	OUT

DATE	DETAILS	CATEGORY	AMOUNT	
			IN	OUT

Totals .... IN .... OUT .... DIFFERENCE

Spending breakdown		Notes
CATEGORY	SUBTOTAL	

WEEKLY BUDGET DIARY

✶ Week Twenty-One ✶

Week beginning	Balances			
	CURRENT ACCOUNT	CREDIT CARDS	SAVINGS	DEBTS
My money mood ☺ 😐 ☹				

Targets _____ IN _____ OUT _____

DATE	DETAILS	CATEGORY	AMOUNT	
			IN	OUT

DATE	DETAILS	CATEGORY	AMOUNT	
			IN	OUT

Totals _____ IN _____ OUT _____ DIFFERENCE

Spending breakdown | Notes

CATEGORY	SUBTOTAL

WEEKLY BUDGET DIARY

✳ Week Twenty-Two ✳

Week beginning	Balances			
	CURRENT ACCOUNT	CREDIT CARDS	SAVINGS	DEBTS
My money mood 🙂 😐 ☹️				

Targets _____ IN _____ OUT

DATE	DETAILS	CATEGORY	AMOUNT	
			IN	OUT

DATE	DETAILS	CATEGORY	AMOUNT	
			IN	OUT

Totals _____ IN _____ OUT _____ DIFFERENCE

Spending breakdown		Notes
CATEGORY	SUBTOTAL	

WEEKLY BUDGET DIARY

✶ Week Twenty-Three ✶

Week beginning	Balances			
	CURRENT ACCOUNT	CREDIT CARDS	SAVINGS	DEBTS
My money mood ☺ 😐 ☹				

Targets _____ IN _____ OUT _____

DATE	DETAILS	CATEGORY	AMOUNT	
			IN	OUT

DATE	DETAILS	CATEGORY	AMOUNT	
			IN	OUT

Totals   IN   OUT   DIFFERENCE

Spending breakdown		Notes
CATEGORY	SUBTOTAL	

WEEKLY BUDGET DIARY

✶ Week Twenty-Four ✶

Week beginning	Balances			
	CURRENT ACCOUNT	CREDIT CARDS	SAVINGS	DEBTS
My money mood ☺ 😐 ☹				

Targets .... IN .... OUT

DATE	DETAILS	CATEGORY	AMOUNT	
			IN	OUT

DATE	DETAILS	CATEGORY	AMOUNT	
			IN	OUT

Totals _____ IN _____ OUT _____ DIFFERENCE

Spending breakdown

CATEGORY	SUBTOTAL

Notes

WEEKLY BUDGET DIARY

Week Twenty-Five

Week beginning	Balances			
	CURRENT ACCOUNT	CREDIT CARDS	SAVINGS	DEBTS
My money mood				

Targets IN OUT

DATE	DETAILS	CATEGORY	AMOUNT	
			IN	OUT

DATE	DETAILS	CATEGORY	AMOUNT	
			IN	OUT

Totals .... IN .... OUT .... DIFFERENCE

Spending breakdown		Notes
CATEGORY	SUBTOTAL	

Week Twenty-Six

Week beginning	Balances			
	CURRENT ACCOUNT	CREDIT CARDS	SAVINGS	DEBTS
My money mood ☺ 😐 ☹				

Targets   IN   OUT

DATE	DETAILS	CATEGORY	AMOUNT	
			IN	OUT

DATE	DETAILS	CATEGORY	AMOUNT	
			IN	OUT

Totals _____ IN _____ OUT _____ DIFFERENCE

Spending breakdown		Notes
CATEGORY	SUBTOTAL	

WEEKLY BUDGET DIARY

✳ Week Twenty-Seven ✳

Week beginning	Balances			
	CURRENT ACCOUNT	CREDIT CARDS	SAVINGS	DEBTS
My money mood 🙂 😐 🙁				

Targets _____ IN _____ OUT

DATE	DETAILS	CATEGORY	AMOUNT	
			IN	OUT

DATE	DETAILS	CATEGORY	AMOUNT	
			IN	OUT

Totals .... IN .... OUT .... DIFFERENCE

Spending breakdown		Notes
CATEGORY	SUBTOTAL	

WEEKLY BUDGET DIARY

✷ Week Twenty-Eight ✷

Week beginning	Balances			
	CURRENT ACCOUNT	CREDIT CARDS	SAVINGS	DEBTS
My money mood ☺ 😐 ☹				

Targets _____ IN _____ OUT _____

DATE	DETAILS	CATEGORY	AMOUNT	
			IN	OUT

DATE	DETAILS	CATEGORY	AMOUNT	
			IN	OUT

Totals _____ IN _____ OUT _____ DIFFERENCE

Spending breakdown		Notes
CATEGORY	SUBTOTAL	

WEEKLY BUDGET DIARY

✴ Week Twenty-Nine ✴

Week beginning	Balances			
	CURRENT ACCOUNT	CREDIT CARDS	SAVINGS	DEBTS
My money mood 🙂 😐 🙁				

Targets _____ IN _____ OUT

DATE	DETAILS	CATEGORY	AMOUNT IN	AMOUNT OUT

DATE	DETAILS	CATEGORY	AMOUNT	
			IN	OUT

Totals _____ IN _____ OUT _____ DIFFERENCE

Spending breakdown

CATEGORY	SUBTOTAL

Notes

WEEKLY BUDGET DIARY

✳ Week Thirty ✳

Week beginning	Balances			
	CURRENT ACCOUNT	CREDIT CARDS	SAVINGS	DEBTS
My money mood				
☺ ☹ ☹				

Targets _____ IN _____ OUT

DATE	DETAILS	CATEGORY	AMOUNT	
			IN	OUT

DATE	DETAILS	CATEGORY	AMOUNT	
			IN	OUT

Totals .... IN .... OUT .... DIFFERENCE

Spending breakdown		Notes
CATEGORY	SUBTOTAL	

WEEKLY BUDGET DIARY

✳ Week Thirty-One ✳

Week beginning	Balances			
	CURRENT ACCOUNT	CREDIT CARDS	SAVINGS	DEBTS
My money mood ☺ 😐 ☹				

Targets   IN   OUT

DATE	DETAILS	CATEGORY	AMOUNT	
			IN	OUT

DATE	DETAILS	CATEGORY	AMOUNT	
			IN	OUT

Totals   IN   OUT   DIFFERENCE

Spending breakdown		Notes
CATEGORY	SUBTOTAL	

WEEKLY BUDGET DIARY

Week Thirty-Two

Week beginning	Balances			
	CURRENT ACCOUNT	CREDIT CARDS	SAVINGS	DEBTS
My money mood ☺ 😐 ☹				

Targets _____ IN _____ OUT

DATE	DETAILS	CATEGORY	AMOUNT	
			IN	OUT

DATE	DETAILS	CATEGORY	AMOUNT	
			IN	OUT

Totals _____ IN _____ OUT _____ DIFFERENCE

Spending breakdown

CATEGORY	SUBTOTAL

Notes

WEEKLY BUDGET DIARY

✶ Week Thirty-Three ✶

Week beginning	Balances			
	CURRENT ACCOUNT	CREDIT CARDS	SAVINGS	DEBTS
My money mood ☺ 😐 ☹				

Targets   IN   OUT

DATE	DETAILS	CATEGORY	AMOUNT	
			IN	OUT

DATE	DETAILS	CATEGORY	AMOUNT	
			IN	OUT

Totals _____ IN _____ OUT _____ DIFFERENCE

Spending breakdown		Notes
CATEGORY	SUBTOTAL	

WEEKLY BUDGET DIARY

✦ Week Thirty-Four ✦

Week beginning	Balances			
	CURRENT ACCOUNT	CREDIT CARDS	SAVINGS	DEBTS
My money mood ☺ 😐 ☹				

Targets   IN   OUT

DATE	DETAILS	CATEGORY	AMOUNT	
			IN	OUT

DATE	DETAILS	CATEGORY	AMOUNT	
			IN	OUT

Totals _____ IN _____ OUT _____ DIFFERENCE

Spending breakdown		Notes
CATEGORY	SUBTOTAL	

WEEKLY BUDGET DIARY

✦ Week Thirty-Five ✦

Week beginning	Balances			
	CURRENT ACCOUNT	CREDIT CARDS	SAVINGS	DEBTS
My money mood ☺ 😐 ☹				

Targets _____ IN _____ OUT

DATE	DETAILS	CATEGORY	AMOUNT	
			IN	OUT

DATE	DETAILS	CATEGORY	AMOUNT	
			IN	OUT

Totals _____ IN _____ OUT _____ DIFFERENCE

Spending breakdown

CATEGORY	SUBTOTAL

Notes

WEEKLY BUDGET DIARY

✶ Week Thirty-Six ✶

Week beginning	Balances			
	CURRENT ACCOUNT	CREDIT CARDS	SAVINGS	DEBTS
My money mood 🙂 😐 🙁				

Targets .... IN .... OUT

DATE	DETAILS	CATEGORY	AMOUNT	
			IN	OUT

DATE	DETAILS	CATEGORY	AMOUNT	
			IN	OUT

Totals _____ IN _____ OUT _____ DIFFERENCE

Spending breakdown		Notes
CATEGORY	SUBTOTAL	

WEEKLY BUDGET DIARY

✱ Week Thirty-Seven ✱

Week beginning	Balances			
	CURRENT ACCOUNT	CREDIT CARDS	SAVINGS	DEBTS
My money mood ☺ 😐 ☹				

Targets _____ IN _____ OUT

DATE	DETAILS	CATEGORY	AMOUNT	
			IN	OUT

DATE	DETAILS	CATEGORY	AMOUNT	
			IN	OUT

Totals _____ IN _____ OUT _____ DIFFERENCE

Spending breakdown		Notes
CATEGORY	SUBTOTAL	

⋆ Week Thirty-Eight ⋆

Week beginning	Balances			
	CURRENT ACCOUNT	CREDIT CARDS	SAVINGS	DEBTS
My money mood ☺ 😐 ☹				

Targets _____ IN _____ OUT

DATE	DETAILS	CATEGORY	AMOUNT	
			IN	OUT

DATE	DETAILS	CATEGORY	AMOUNT	
			IN	OUT

Totals   IN   OUT   DIFFERENCE

Spending breakdown		Notes
CATEGORY	SUBTOTAL	

WEEKLY BUDGET DIARY

Week Thirty-Nine

Week beginning	Balances			
	CURRENT ACCOUNT	CREDIT CARDS	SAVINGS	DEBTS
My money mood ☺ 😐 ☹				

Targets _____ IN _____ OUT _____

DATE	DETAILS	CATEGORY	AMOUNT	
			IN	OUT

DATE	DETAILS	CATEGORY	AMOUNT	
			IN	OUT

Totals _____ IN _____ OUT _____ DIFFERENCE

Spending breakdown		Notes
CATEGORY	SUBTOTAL	

WEEKLY BUDGET DIARY

✳ Week Forty ✳

Week beginning	Balances			
	CURRENT ACCOUNT	CREDIT CARDS	SAVINGS	DEBTS
My money mood ☺ 😐 ☹				

Targets _____ IN _____ OUT

DATE	DETAILS	CATEGORY	AMOUNT	
			IN	OUT

DATE	DETAILS	CATEGORY	AMOUNT	
			IN	OUT

Totals _____ IN _____ OUT _____ DIFFERENCE

Spending breakdown

CATEGORY	SUBTOTAL

Notes

WEEKLY BUDGET DIARY

✶ Week Forty-One ✶

Week beginning	Balances			
	CURRENT ACCOUNT	CREDIT CARDS	SAVINGS	DEBTS
My money mood 🙂 😐 🙁				

Targets — IN — OUT

DATE	DETAILS	CATEGORY	AMOUNT	
			IN	OUT

DATE	DETAILS	CATEGORY	AMOUNT	
			IN	OUT

Totals _____ IN _____ OUT _____ DIFFERENCE

Spending breakdown | Notes

CATEGORY	SUBTOTAL

WEEKLY BUDGET DIARY

✳ Week Forty-Two ✳

Week beginning	Balances			
	CURRENT ACCOUNT	CREDIT CARDS	SAVINGS	DEBTS
My money mood ☺ 😐 ☹				

Targets _____ IN _____ OUT _____

DATE	DETAILS	CATEGORY	AMOUNT	
			IN	OUT

DATE	DETAILS	CATEGORY	AMOUNT	
			IN	OUT

Totals _____ IN _____ OUT _____ DIFFERENCE

Spending breakdown		Notes
CATEGORY	SUBTOTAL	

Weekly Budget Diary

Week Forty-Three

Week beginning	Balances			
	CURRENT ACCOUNT	CREDIT CARDS	SAVINGS	DEBTS
My money mood ☺ 😐 ☹				

Targets _____ IN _____ OUT

DATE	DETAILS	CATEGORY	AMOUNT	
			IN	OUT

DATE	DETAILS	CATEGORY	AMOUNT	
			IN	OUT

Totals _____ IN _____ OUT _____ DIFFERENCE

Spending breakdown		Notes
CATEGORY	SUBTOTAL	

WEEKLY BUDGET DIARY

✦ Week Forty-Four ✦

Week beginning	Balances			
	CURRENT ACCOUNT	CREDIT CARDS	SAVINGS	DEBTS
My money mood ☺ 😐 ☹				

Targets _____ IN _____ OUT

DATE	DETAILS	CATEGORY	AMOUNT IN	AMOUNT OUT

DATE	DETAILS	CATEGORY	AMOUNT	
			IN	OUT

Totals _____ IN _____ OUT _____ DIFFERENCE

Spending breakdown		Notes
CATEGORY	SUBTOTAL	

WEEKLY BUDGET DIARY

Week Forty-Five

Week beginning	Balances			
	CURRENT ACCOUNT	CREDIT CARDS	SAVINGS	DEBTS
My money mood ☺ 😐 ☹				

Targets   IN   OUT

DATE	DETAILS	CATEGORY	AMOUNT	
			IN	OUT

DATE	DETAILS	CATEGORY	AMOUNT	
			IN	OUT

Totals _____ IN _____ OUT _____ DIFFERENCE

Spending breakdown		Notes
CATEGORY	SUBTOTAL	

WEEKLY BUDGET DIARY

Week Forty-Six

Week beginning	Balances			
	CURRENT ACCOUNT	CREDIT CARDS	SAVINGS	DEBTS
My money mood ☺ 😐 ☹				

Targets _____ IN _____ OUT

DATE	DETAILS	CATEGORY	AMOUNT	
			IN	OUT

DATE	DETAILS	CATEGORY	AMOUNT	
			IN	OUT

Totals .... IN .... OUT .... DIFFERENCE

Spending breakdown		Notes
CATEGORY	SUBTOTAL	

WEEKLY BUDGET DIARY

Week Forty-Seven

Week beginning	Balances			
	CURRENT ACCOUNT	CREDIT CARDS	SAVINGS	DEBTS
My money mood :) :| :(				

Targets _____ IN _____ OUT

DATE	DETAILS	CATEGORY	AMOUNT	
			IN	OUT

DATE	DETAILS	CATEGORY	AMOUNT	
			IN	OUT

Totals _____ IN _____ OUT _____ DIFFERENCE

Spending breakdown		Notes
CATEGORY	SUBTOTAL	

WEEKLY BUDGET DIARY

Week Forty-Eight

Week beginning	Balances			
	CURRENT ACCOUNT	CREDIT CARDS	SAVINGS	DEBTS
My money mood ☺ 😐 ☹				

Targets _____ IN _____ OUT _____

DATE	DETAILS	CATEGORY	AMOUNT	
			IN	OUT

DATE	DETAILS	CATEGORY	AMOUNT	
			IN	OUT

Totals _____ IN _____ OUT _____ DIFFERENCE

Spending breakdown		Notes
CATEGORY	SUBTOTAL	

Week Forty-Nine

Week beginning	Balances				
	CURRENT ACCOUNT	CREDIT CARDS	SAVINGS	DEBTS
My money mood ☺ 😐 ☹				

Targets _____ IN _____ OUT

DATE	DETAILS	CATEGORY	AMOUNT	
			IN	OUT

DATE	DETAILS	CATEGORY	AMOUNT	
			IN	OUT

Totals _____ IN _____ OUT _____ DIFFERENCE

Spending breakdown

CATEGORY	SUBTOTAL

Notes

WEEKLY BUDGET DIARY

Week Fifty

Week beginning	Balances			
	CURRENT ACCOUNT	CREDIT CARDS	SAVINGS	DEBTS
My money mood ☺ 😐 ☹				

Targets _____ IN _____ OUT _____

DATE	DETAILS	CATEGORY	AMOUNT	
			IN	OUT

DATE	DETAILS	CATEGORY	AMOUNT	
			IN	OUT

Totals   IN   OUT   DIFFERENCE

Spending breakdown		Notes
CATEGORY	SUBTOTAL	

Week Fifty-One

Week beginning	Balances				
	CURRENT ACCOUNT	CREDIT CARDS	SAVINGS	DEBTS
My money mood ☺ 😐 ☹				

Targets   IN   OUT

DATE	DETAILS	CATEGORY	AMOUNT	
			IN	OUT

DATE	DETAILS	CATEGORY	AMOUNT	
			IN	OUT

Totals   IN   OUT   DIFFERENCE

Spending breakdown		Notes
CATEGORY	SUBTOTAL	

WEEKLY BUDGET DIARY

✶ Week Fifty-Two ✶

Week beginning	Balances			
	CURRENT ACCOUNT	CREDIT CARDS	SAVINGS	DEBTS
My money mood ☺ 😐 ☹				

Targets _____ IN _____ OUT

DATE	DETAILS	CATEGORY	AMOUNT	
			IN	OUT

DATE	DETAILS	CATEGORY	AMOUNT	
			IN	OUT

Totals   IN   OUT   DIFFERENCE

Spending breakdown		Notes
CATEGORY	SUBTOTAL	

Review & Reflect

140   HOW TO COMPLETE THE MONTHLY TOTALS
A guide to using the spending review section

142   YOUR MONTHLY TOTALS
Monitor your finances at the end of each month

166   ANNUAL REVIEW
Analyse your overall spending for the year

172   REFLECT ON YOUR PROGRESS
Contemplate the impact of your new budgeting habits

SPENDING REVIEWS

How to complete the monthly totals

Use the following pages to collate your overall income and outgoings at the end of each month.
Here are some tips on how to complete each section…

1 MAIN TABLE

Use the information from your weekly journal entries for the month to complete the table. For most weeks, you can use the category subtotals from the spending breakdown sections. However, for weeks that span consecutive months, you may have to refer to the individual entries of your weekly diary.

2 TOTALS

Calculate the total income and outgoings. Subtract the 'out' from the 'in' value to find your net income – a negative value shows you spent more than you earned.

> **Money is only a tool. It will take you wherever you wish, but it will not replace you as the driver**
>
> — AYN RAND

At the end of the year, you can use the information from your monthly totals to help compile your annual spending review (starting on page 166).

Monthly spending review

Total spent this month

ESSENTIAL	NON-ESSENTIAL

Most expensive categories this month

ESSENTIAL	NON-ESSENTIAL

My successes this month

Have I stuck to my budgets this month? If not, why not?

My plan or target for next month

Notes

3 ESSENTIALS VS NON-ESSENTIALS

Add up your spend in all the essential categories and then compare this to the total for your non-essentials. Also take note of the categories you have spent the most on this month.

4 REVIEW YOUR MONTH

Take a moment to consider these prompts and assess your spending and saving habits throughout the month.

5 NOTES

Use this section to add any comments or reminders for the month, or to use as extra space for any of the other sections if you run out of room.

YOUR MONTHLY TOTALS

✷ Month One ✷

JAN   FEB   MAR   [APR   MAY]   JUN   JUL   AUG   SEP   OCT   NOV   DEC

CATEGORY	ESSENTIAL Y/N	AMOUNT IN	AMOUNT OUT

Totals   IN   OUT   DIFFERENCE

Monthly spending review

Total spent this month

ESSENTIAL	NON-ESSENTIAL

Most expensive categories this month

ESSENTIAL	NON-ESSENTIAL

My successes this month

Have I stuck to my budgets this month? If not, why not?

My plan or target for next month

Notes

YOUR MONTHLY TOTALS

✦ Month Two ✦

JAN FEB MAR APR MAY JUN JUL AUG SEP OCT NOV DEC

CATEGORY	ESSENTIAL Y/N	AMOUNT	
		IN	OUT

Totals   IN   OUT   DIFFERENCE

Monthly spending review

Total spent this month

ESSENTIAL	NON-ESSENTIAL

Most expensive categories this month

ESSENTIAL	NON-ESSENTIAL

My successes this month

Have I stuck to my budgets this month? If not, why not?

My plan or target for next month

Notes

YOUR MONTHLY TOTALS

✶ Month Three ✶

JAN FEB MAR APR MAY JUN JUL AUG SEP OCT NOV DEC

CATEGORY	ESSENTIAL Y/N	AMOUNT IN	OUT

Totals .... IN .... OUT .... DIFFERENCE

Monthly spending review

Total spent this month

ESSENTIAL	NON-ESSENTIAL

Most expensive categories this month

ESSENTIAL	NON-ESSENTIAL

My successes this month

Have I stuck to my budgets this month? If not, why not?

My plan or target for next month

Notes

YOUR MONTHLY TOTALS

✶ Month Four ✶

JAN FEB MAR APR MAY JUN JUL AUG SEP OCT NOV DEC

CATEGORY	ESSENTIAL Y/N	AMOUNT IN	OUT

Totals   IN   OUT   DIFFERENCE

Monthly spending review

Total spent this month	
ESSENTIAL	NON-ESSENTIAL

Most expensive categories this month	
ESSENTIAL	NON-ESSENTIAL

My successes this month

Have I stuck to my budgets this month? If not, why not?

My plan or target for next month

Notes

YOUR MONTHLY TOTALS

Month Five

JAN FEB MAR APR MAY JUN JUL AUG SEP OCT NOV DEC

CATEGORY	ESSENTIAL Y/N	AMOUNT IN	AMOUNT OUT

Totals   IN   OUT   DIFFERENCE

Monthly spending review

Total spent this month

ESSENTIAL	NON-ESSENTIAL

Most expensive categories this month

ESSENTIAL	NON-ESSENTIAL

My successes this month

Have I stuck to my budgets this month? If not, why not?

My plan or target for next month

Notes

YOUR MONTHLY TOTALS

✷ Month Six ✷

JAN FEB MAR APR MAY JUN JUL AUG SEP OCT NOV DEC

CATEGORY	ESSENTIAL Y/N	AMOUNT IN	AMOUNT OUT

Totals   IN   OUT   DIFFERENCE

Monthly spending review

Total spent this month

ESSENTIAL	NON-ESSENTIAL

Most expensive categories this month

ESSENTIAL	NON-ESSENTIAL

My successes this month

Have I stuck to my budgets this month? If not, why not?

My plan or target for next month

Notes

YOUR MONTHLY TOTALS

Month Seven

| JAN | FEB | MAR | APR | MAY | JUN | JUL | AUG | SEP | OCT | NOV | DEC |

CATEGORY	ESSENTIAL Y/N	AMOUNT	
		IN	OUT

Totals   IN   OUT   DIFFERENCE

Monthly spending review

Total spent this month

ESSENTIAL	NON-ESSENTIAL

Most expensive categories this month

ESSENTIAL	NON-ESSENTIAL

My successes this month

Have I stuck to my budgets this month? If not, why not?

My plan or target for next month

Notes

YOUR MONTHLY TOTALS

✶ Month Eight ✶

JAN FEB MAR APR MAY JUN JUL AUG SEP OCT NOV DEC

CATEGORY	ESSENTIAL Y/N	AMOUNT IN	OUT

Totals   IN _____   OUT _____   DIFFERENCE _____

Monthly spending review

Total spent this month

ESSENTIAL	NON-ESSENTIAL

Most expensive categories this month

ESSENTIAL	NON-ESSENTIAL

My successes this month

Have I stuck to my budgets this month? If not, why not?

My plan or target for next month

Notes

Your Monthly Totals

✶ Month Nine ✶

JAN FEB MAR APR MAY JUN JUL AUG SEP OCT NOV DEC

CATEGORY	ESSENTIAL Y/N	AMOUNT IN	OUT

Totals   IN   OUT   DIFFERENCE

Monthly spending review

Total spent this month

ESSENTIAL	NON-ESSENTIAL

Most expensive categories this month

ESSENTIAL	NON-ESSENTIAL

My successes this month

Have I stuck to my budgets this month? If not, why not?

My plan or target for next month

Notes

YOUR MONTHLY TOTALS

Month Ten

JAN　FEB　MAR　APR　MAY　JUN　JUL　AUG　SEP　OCT　NOV　DEC

CATEGORY	ESSENTIAL Y/N	AMOUNT IN	AMOUNT OUT

Totals　　　IN　　　OUT　　　DIFFERENCE

Monthly spending review

Total spent this month

ESSENTIAL	NON-ESSENTIAL

Most expensive categories this month

ESSENTIAL	NON-ESSENTIAL

My successes this month

Have I stuck to my budgets this month? If not, why not?

My plan or target for next month

Notes

YOUR MONTHLY TOTALS

✶ Month Eleven ✶

JAN FEB MAR APR MAY JUN JUL AUG SEP OCT NOV DEC

CATEGORY	ESSENTIAL Y/N	AMOUNT IN	AMOUNT OUT

Totals   IN   OUT   DIFFERENCE

Monthly spending review

Total spent this month

ESSENTIAL	NON-ESSENTIAL

Most expensive categories this month

ESSENTIAL	NON-ESSENTIAL

My successes this month

Have I stuck to my budgets this month? If not, why not?

My plan or target for next month

Notes

YOUR MONTHLY TOTALS

✦ Month Twelve ✦

JAN FEB MAR APR MAY JUN JUL AUG SEP OCT NOV DEC

CATEGORY	ESSENTIAL Y/N	AMOUNT	
		IN	OUT

Totals   IN   OUT   DIFFERENCE

Monthly spending review

Total spent this month

ESSENTIAL	NON-ESSENTIAL

Most expensive categories this month

ESSENTIAL	NON-ESSENTIAL

My successes this month

Have I stuck to my budgets this month? If not, why not?

My plan or target for next month

Notes

SPENDING REVIEWS

✳ Annual review ✳

Look back through your completed entries for each month (pages 142-165) and use this table to collate all your spending totals. This will show how much you are really spending on each category over the course of a year.

Categories	Example Category 1	Example Category 2						
Essential? (Tick)	✓	✗						
JANUARY	25	10						
FEBRUARY	30	0						
MARCH	20	15						
APRIL	35	15						
MAY	40	20						
JUNE	20	0						
JULY	30	10						
AUGUST	20	15						
SEPTEMBER	30	10						
OCTOBER	50	0						
NOVEMBER	30	0						
DECEMBER	30	15						
Totals	360	110						

NOTES

> The table is continued over the page if you need to include more categories

NOTES

Categories								
Essential? (Tick)								
JANUARY								
FEBRUARY								
MARCH								
APRIL								
MAY								
JUNE								
JULY								
AUGUST								
SEPTEMBER								
OCTOBER								
NOVEMBER								
DECEMBER								
Totals								

TOTAL SPEND THIS YEAR

Combine the totals listed in the table for all your essential and non-essential categories.

ESSENTIAL _____   NON-ESSENTIAL _____

Use the following table to compare your account balances for the start and end of your journaling year. Then, follow the prompts on the right to reflect on your progress.

Balances	Year Start	Year End	DIFFERENCE
CURRENT ACCOUNT			
SAVINGS & INVESTMENTS			
CREDIT CARDS			
DEBTS			
OTHER			

> **Budgeting your money is the key to having enough**
> — ELIZABETH WARREN

My successes this year

What has been challenging?

What could I improve next year?

Notes

REVIEW & REFLECT

✳ Reflect on ✳ your progress

Look back over your last year of budgeting. Think about what's gone well and what could be improved

Well done for getting to the end of your year-long journey through the world of budgeting. We hope that you've found this journal to be a useful tool for logging your spending, creating some new habits and learning a few tricks along the way.

Before you rush into the next 12 months, we encourage you to take a moment to look back over the last period. This chance to reflect gives you the opportunity to review your habits and make any changes to your goals in the future.

First, make sure that you have filled in your monthly and annual totals in the previous pages. This will give you a clear picture of your whole year. Take some time to go over your spendings and savings, and make sure that all of your data is as accurate as possible. At a first glance, see if there are any patterns that you notice. For example, are there any months where you have spent significantly more or less than others? This might be due to a spate of birthdays or a big holiday where you've spent more than normal, or you might have quieter months in winter where you go out less. Identifying these spending patterns is very useful when planning your budget and goals for the year ahead, as you can allow for the more expensive times, and perhaps even set aside more savings to cover the big-money months if you need to.

> ❞ Identifying your spending patterns is useful when planning your budget and goals for the next year ❞

CATEGORY BREAKDOWNS

Take a look at all of your category spending totals
for the year, and consider the following:

My most expensive categories:

ESSENTIAL   VALUE
....

NON-ESSENTIAL   VALUE
....

Did the total spend for any categories surprise you?

....

....

Is your non-essential spending pushing your budget over the limit? If so, what areas can you cut back on?

....

....

Notes

....

....

> **❝ If you feel more in control of your finances, then don't forget to congratulate yourself ❞**

    Also look at the different categories that you set up. You may see more patterns here. When you see a total for a category, it might come as a surprise – did you realise how much you were spending in some areas? Or are you pleased that a category you thought would be higher is much lower? We've given you some space in this section to write down your thoughts about these category totals, which again can be a handy exercise to help you review this year before planning for the next.

    When you have the totals in front of you, you have the opportunity to check in on your goals for the year. Flick back to the front of this journal and read the goals you set for the short, medium and long term. Now is a good time to see how you've done. Use the space provided to write down your current goals, your targets and your progress towards those targets. You can also add any specific comments on your progress, such as whether you're ahead of your target, or maybe an unexpected event has meant you've had to change your goal.

    With it all written down, you can analyse your goal progress a little more. Have you met any targets that you intended to complete by the end of the year? If you haven't, then what do you think is responsible for this? For longer-term or ongoing goals, think about whether you need to make any adjustments going forwards to help you achieve these, or whether you need to amend your targets.

    Another thing that you might want to reflect on is whether you have changed any 'bad' money habits or introduced any new 'good' money habits. Take a glance back at our section on 'What type of spender are you?' and think about the spending personality (or personalities) you identified with the most. Do you think that these still reflect your behaviour as a spender now, or have your habits changed? If you feel like your spending habits are broadly the same, now might be the time to think about setting some goals around habits you'd like to break for the next year. However, if you feel you've improved your spending habits and feel more in control of your finances, then don't forget to congratulate yourself. This is a huge achievement and one that you should take credit for. It can be really difficult to undo years of impulsive spending, for example, and it's not easy to change things that are so ingrained. In the 'Final thoughts' section at the end of this journal, use the 'notes' space to write down any big changes you've made to the way you approach your money.

Learning how to manage finances and save isn't something that we're always taught at school, so you can't expect to know everything. There will still be a lot to learn, but we hope you've picked up some useful tools and resources along the way. Think about what has gone particularly well this year – this could be anything from meeting a goal, feeling more prepared for big events, being able to free up

MY PROGRESS

Look back at your goals (from page 23). What progress have you made towards them over the past year? You may prefer to focus on your short-term and ongoing goals at this stage.

Goal	Target value (If applicable)	Value achieved so far	Comments
Example: Pay off remaining car lease	£8,000	£4,250	Getting there! Should be paid off by this time next year

more money for a holiday, not using a credit card, creating an emergency fund, or breaking a daily takeaway coffee habit. Have you set up any systems that have been helpful? For example, this could be designating separate savings pots, creating a spreadsheet to track progress towards a goal, or using this journal to note down your daily spends.

Equally, it's important to think about what hasn't gone so well. Don't be too hard on yourself; this isn't about being downhearted if you haven't managed everything you wanted to. Maybe the goals were set too high, or maybe things happened that you couldn't prepare for. These are all important lessons that will help you to plan for the next year. Be honest about anything you feel has hampered your financial progress this year, as this will enable you to realistically review your situation.

After this period of reflection, the next step is to think about what you want to do to keep up the good work in the future. Where could you make improvements next time? What habits would you like to keep and what habits would you like to work on a little more? Have you come across any other resources that you might like to introduce in the next year?

The key to maintaining your good habits and hard work comes from looking back and seeing how far you've come. It can feel difficult in the moment to stick to a budget, especially if it's the first time you have ever tried to do something like this. However, seeing the end results of all your effort can make it worthwhile and incentivise you to continue. This is why it's important not to set unachievable goals or cut back on your spending too heavy-handedly – you want to be able to manage your finances for years to come without feeling deprived. This is about a way of life, not just a short-term solution.

Final thoughts

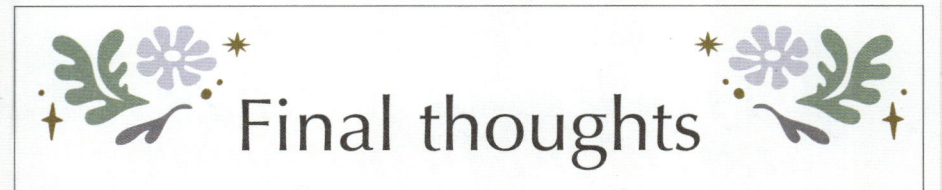

Consider the following statements – how well do they reflect your current situation after using this journal? Use the space below to jot down any other thoughts or feelings you have about your experience over the past year.

I am in a better position financially now than when I started this journal

STRONGLY DISAGREE   DISAGREE   NEUTRAL   AGREE   STRONGLY AGREE

I feel more in control of my money

STRONGLY DISAGREE   DISAGREE   NEUTRAL   AGREE   STRONGLY AGREE

I have achieved, or am making good progress towards, one or more of my financial goals

STRONGLY DISAGREE   DISAGREE   NEUTRAL   AGREE   STRONGLY AGREE

I have reduced or eliminated my 'bad' money habits

STRONGLY DISAGREE   DISAGREE   NEUTRAL   AGREE   STRONGLY AGREE

I have developed a strong set of 'good' money habits

STRONGLY DISAGREE   DISAGREE   NEUTRAL   AGREE   STRONGLY AGREE

Notes

ON SALE NOW!

Track your feelings and identify patterns

Build a complete picture of the mood influences in your life – record information on your sleep, diet, physical health, mental health and much more. Look at how these factors affect how you feel in order to make small changes to improve your moods.

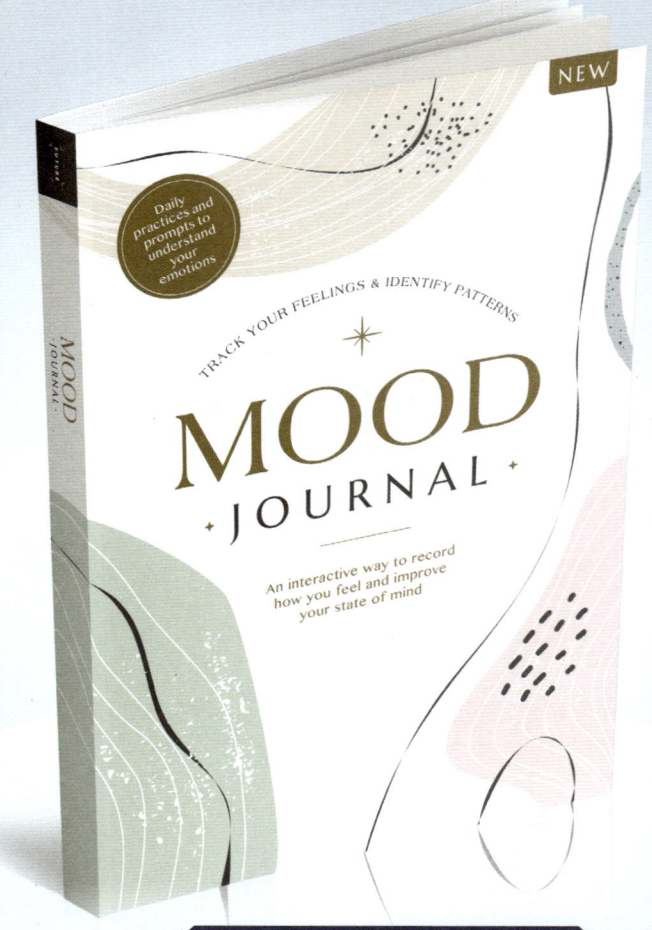

NEW

Daily practices and prompts to understand your emotions

TRACK YOUR FEELINGS & IDENTIFY PATTERNS

MOOD JOURNAL

An interactive way to record how you feel and improve your state of mind

Ordering is easy. Go online at:
WWW.MAGAZINESDIRECT.COM
Or get it from selected supermarkets & newsagents

FUTURE